Strange ... But True?

HAUNTED PLACES

ELIZABETH NOLL

BLACK
RABBIT
BOOKS

Bolt is published by Black Rabbit Books
P.O. Box 3263, Mankato, Minnesota, 56002.
www.blackrabbitbooks.com
Copyright © 2017 Black Rabbit Books

Design and Production by Michael Sellner
Photo Research by Rhonda Milbrett

Library of Congress Control Number: 2015954851

HC ISBN: 978-1-68072-025-9   PB ISBN: 978-1-68072-294-9

Printed in the United States at CG Book Printers,
North Mankato, Minnesota, 56003. PO #1795 4/16

Contents

CHAPTER 1

A  Mansion

The air was still as a **tourist** wandered through the LaLaurie House. Suddenly, a scream broke the silence. Then, he heard a cracking whip. He peeked around a corner. No one was there.

5

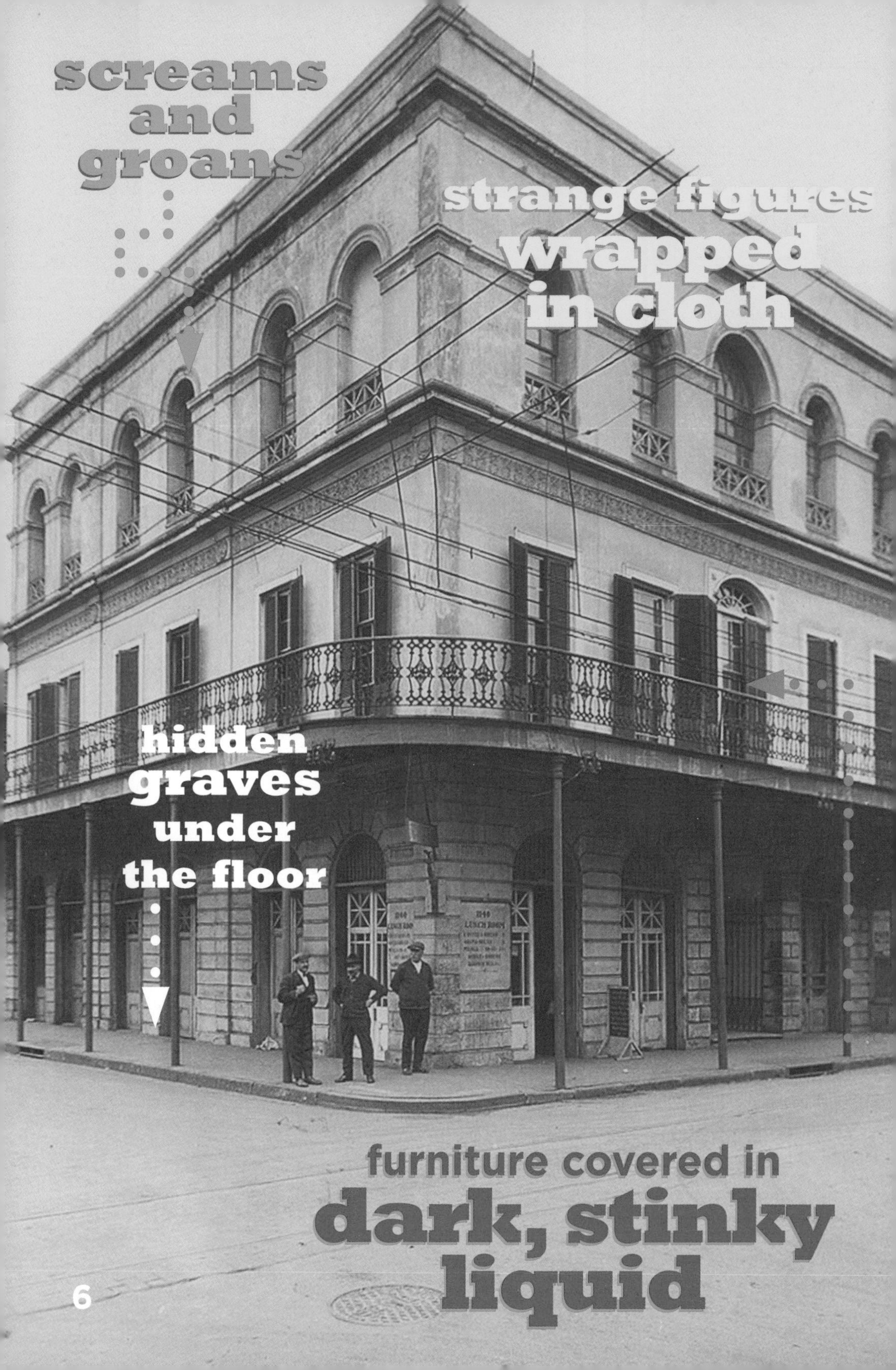

screams
and
groans

strange figures
wrapped
in cloth

hidden
graves
under
the floor

furniture covered in
dark, stinky
liquid

An Evil History

In the 1830s, Mrs. LaLaurie and her husband owned the house. In secret, she whipped her **slaves** and locked them in the attic. She chained the cook to the stove.

Today, many people say they have heard screams in the house. They think the noises come from the slaves' ghosts.

Mysterious Events

People claim to see and hear odd things at the LaLaurie House.

CHAPTER 2

Seeing

Stories of haunted places are found all around the world. Many people believe ghosts live in places where bad events happened. But others think the stories are made up.

Alcatraz is a famous prison. It's also a famous spot for ghosts. About 28 men died at the prison before it closed. Visitors today say they hear whispering voices. Guards have seen white **figures** walk the halls.

FAMOUS HAUNTED PLACES

HALIFAX CITADEL IN NOVA SCOTIA

GETTYSBURG BATTLEFIELD IN PENNSYLVANIA

ISLAND OF THE DOLLS IN XOCHIMILCO, MEXICO

LALAURIE HOUSE IN NEW ORLEANS, LOUISIANA

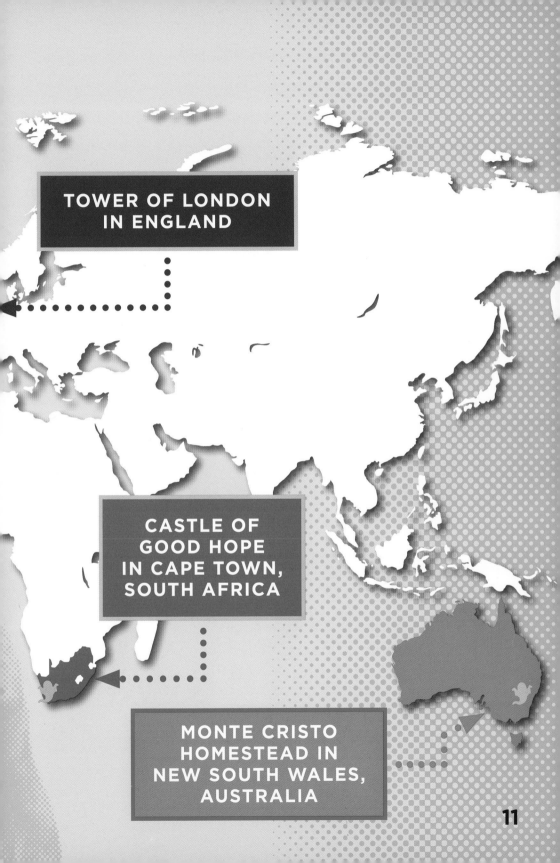

TOWER OF LONDON
IN ENGLAND

CASTLE OF
GOOD HOPE
IN CAPE TOWN,
SOUTH AFRICA

MONTE CRISTO
HOMESTEAD IN
NEW SOUTH WALES,
AUSTRALIA

63%
don't
believe

37%
believe

The White House

Some people call the White House the most haunted house in the United States. Many say they've seen Abraham Lincoln's ghost. In the stories, he is usually in his bedroom or the Oval Office. Others say they've seen the ghost of first lady Abigail Adams. President Andrew Jackson might roam there too.

How Many Believe?

Almost four out of 10 people in the United States believe in haunted houses.

Ghosts of War

In 1863, almost 8,000 people died in the Battle of Gettysburg. Today, many people visit the battlefield in Pennsylvania. Some say they hear the sounds of fighting soldiers. Others have seen ghostly men with **wounds**.

The Battle of Gettysburg took place during the U.S. Civil War. It lasted three days.

CHAPTER 3

Not-So-Haunted

Some places might seem mysterious. But noises and cold spots turn out to be everyday things. In one story, a family heard piano music in their house. But there wasn't a piano. They heard footsteps when no one was there.

Later, someone **investigated**. He found out that a boy played piano nearby. And workers walked on an outside staircase.

The family moved out because they were so scared.

It's Just the Wind

In another story, family members said they heard scraping sounds at night. They also felt freezing cold places in their house. They were sure ghosts lived there. But an investigator found simple answers. The scraping sound was a neighbor raking leaves. Bad windows let in cold air.

WHAT'S GOING ON?

COLD SPOTS

HISTORY OF BAD EVENTS

 Searching for Answers

People have proven some places are not haunted. But other places are still mysteries. Ghost hunters go to places they think are haunted. They try to take pictures of ghosts. They say ghosts show up as circles of light.

Lights, Camera, Action!

Ghost hunters also **record** the sounds in a place. They listen to the recordings after they leave. They say sometimes they hear ghosts talk.

RECORDER

Ghost Hunting Tools

MOTION DETECTOR

PIR MP. ALERT

VIDEO CAMERA

THERMOMETER

Still Mysterious

Researchers study haunted places. They try to figure out what those ghostly figures could be. They say people's brains mistake shadows for ghosts. Odd **reflections** in mirrors could look like ghosts too.

Many people believe ghosts haunt houses and **cemeteries**. They say they've seen or heard them. Others say there's no proof. What do you think?

Believe It or Not?

Answer the questions below.
Then add up your points to
see if you believe.

1 You find yourself by an old cemetery. What do you do?

A. Run! (3 points)

B. Go a little faster and hold your breath. (2 points)

C. Stop and look around. (1 point)

2 Can the brain be fooled by shadows or mirrors?

A. No. My brain knows when something's strange. (3 points)

B. Maybe. (2 points)

C. Definitely. (1 point)

3 You shiver as you walk into an empty room. What do you think?

A. Someone is in here. (3 points)

B. Weird. I wonder why I felt like that. (2 points)

C. A window must be open. (1 point)

. . . .

3 points:
There's no way you think places can be haunted.

4–8 points:
Maybe it's real. But then again, maybe it's not.

9 points:
You're a total believer!

cemetery (SEM-uh-ter-ee)—a place where dead people are buried

figure (FI-guhr)—a person or animal that can only be seen as a shape or outline

investigate (in-VES-tuh-gayt)—to try to find out the facts

record (re-KORD)—to store sounds, images, or other things on a disk or tape so it can be heard or seen later

reflection (ree-FLEK-shun)—an image that is seen in a mirror or shiny surface

slave (SLAYV)—someone who is owned by another person and forced to do work without pay

tourist (TOOR-ist)—a person who travels for fun

wound (WOOND)—an injury that is caused when a knife, bullet, or other thing cuts the skin

BOOKS

Harmon, Daniel E. *Haunted Places and Ghostly Encounters*. The Supernatural. Pittsburgh: Eldorado Ink, 2015.

Lunis, Natalie. *Spooky Schools*. Scary Places. New York: Bearport Pub., 2013.

Parish, Patrick. *Are Haunted Houses Real?* Unexplained: What's the Evidence? Mankato, MN: Amicus High Interest, 2014.

WEBSITES

Ghosts
sd4kids.skepdic.com/ghosts.html

Introduction to Ghost Investigating
kids.ghostvillage.com/jrghosthunters/index.shtml

Where to Go to Sleep in the World's 10 Scariest Haunted Houses
discoverykids.com/parents/where-to-go-to-sleep-in-the-worlds-10-scariest-haunted-houses/

INDEX